**JERMY
STRE
THEATRE**

The Blinding Light

by Howard Brenton

Jermyn Street Theatre, London
6 September–14 October 2017

The Blinding Light was commissioned by Jermyn Street Theatre

Welcome to Jermyn Street Theatre

It's almost a decade since I first came down our stairs to see a play. I knew little about this theatre, and couldn't believe my eyes: a gem of a studio, in the heart of Piccadilly. Not long afterwards, I met Penny Horner to suggest a production of Stephen Sondheim's *Saturday Night*. The show did well – it transferred to the West End, where Sondheim saw it, cried in front of the astonished actors, and gave me notes on Brooklyn accents. I was twenty-four, which makes me cringe now, although – in my defence – Sondheim was even younger when he wrote it.

Saturday Night was followed by *Anyone Can Whistle*, starring Rosalie Craig – who she? – the next year. In 2012, I was back with Howard Brenton's beautiful *Bloody Poetry* – the beginning of a fruitful friendship. In 2013, I revived Graham Greene's *The Living Room* with a cast of impeccable vintage, alongside a dazzling Tuppence Middleton making her stage debut. The next year I directed the first revival of Terence Rattigan's *First Episode*. This theatre has been the backdrop to much of my professional – and my personal – life.

So you can imagine my pleasure and pride when I was asked to take over from Anthony Biggs as Artistic Director. Anthony could not have been kinder or more considerate during our handover period, but my real thanks are due to the woman who founded this theatre with Howard Jameson twenty-three years ago, and remains integral to its continued success: our Executive Director, the indomitable Penny Horner.

Lots is changing. Some of it you'll notice. Much is infrastructural and below the surface. We've recruited an in-house management team for the first time. We're abandoning our old venue-for-hire model to become a producing house. We're paying a modest, but proper, salary to all our actors and production teams. We're committed to employing at least 50% women on- and offstage. We're going to take risks. We need to raise a lot of money, and we think we can.

We think plays matter. We think actors matter. We think ideas matter and emotions matter. We think our audience is up for a new play as well as an old play, a challenge as well as a good time. In a world characterised by 140-character polarities, we think theatre should offer complexity, nuance, provocation – and plenty of laughs.

I don't want to write much about *The Blinding Light* – it's too rich a play for glib commentary here – except thank you to Howard. It's our fourth collaboration and our third with August Strindberg, who might miss the first night but always seems to have plenty to say.

Whether you're an old friend or a new visitor, I hope you'll return to see the rest of the Escape Season.

In my experience, once you've discovered this place, you'll be back.

Tom Littler
Artistic Director

The Blinding Light

by Howard Brenton

Cast

LOLA, *a chambermaid*	Laura Morgan
AUGUST	Jasper Britton
SIRI, *August's first wife*	Susannah Harker
FRIDA, *August's second wife*	Gala Gordon

Creative Team

Director	Tom Littler
Set Designer	Cherry Truluck for Lucky Bert
Costume Designer	Emily Stuart
Lighting Designer	William Reynolds
Composer and Sound Designer	Max Pappenheim
Associate Director	Stella Powell-Jones

A room in the Hotel Orfila, Paris,
February 1896

Meet the Cast

JASPER BRITTON – August

Jasper has most recently appeared in *What the Butler Saw* (Leicester Curve); *The Libertine* (Theatre Royal Bath, Theatre Royal Haymarket). Prior to that, *Richard II*, *The Jew of Malta* and *Henry IV, Parts I and II* (RSC at Stratford, Barbican and New York). His many other credits include *Race* (Hampstead); *The Picture of Dorian Gray* (Abbey); *Who's Afraid of Virginia Woolf?* (Sheffield Crucible); *Fabrication* (The Print Room); *The Last Cigarette* (Chichester Festival Theatre/West End); *Fram* (National Theatre); *Oedipus* (National Theatre); *Rhinoceros* (Royal Court); *The Taming of the Shew* (RSC, Washington DC/West End); *Japes* (Theatre Royal Haymarket); *The Tempest* (Shakespeare's Globe) and *The Visit* (Complicite). Film credits include *Rise of the Footsoldier 2*, *Blood*, *Anonymous*, *Morris: A Life with Bells On* and *The New World*.

GALA GORDON – Frida

Gala trained at Guildhall School of Music and Drama. After graduation, Gala made her professional stage debut in 2012, playing the lead role of Irina in Benedict Andrews' production of Chekhov's *Three Sisters* at the Young Vic, starring opposite Vanessa Kirby. Since then she has appeared in feature films *Kids in Love* and *White Island*. Television credits include *Endeavour* (ITV) and *The Crown* (Netflix).

SUSANNAH HARKER – Siri

Susannah's theatre credits include *Each His Own Wildnerness* (Orange Tree); *The Vortex* (The Gate, Dublin); *Abigail's Party* (The Chocolate Factory/Wyndham's Theatre); *Little Platoons* (Bush Theatre); *A Good Death* (National Theatre Studio); *Lucky Seven* (Hampstead Theatre); *On the Shore of the Wild World* (Royal Exchange Theatre/National Theatre); *Three Sisters* (Playhouse Theatre); *The Browning Version* (Derby Playhouse); *Uncle Vanya* (The Gate/New York); *Tartuffe* (Almeida) and *The Glass Menagerie* (Nottingham Playhouse). Television credits include Jane Bennett in the BBC's adaption of *Pride and Prejudice*, her BAFTA-nominated Mattie Storin in *House of Cards*, *New Tricks*, *Young James*, *Moving On*, *Midsomer Murders*, *Perfect Parents*, *Waking The Dead*, *Murder in Mind – Motive*, *Ultra-Violet*, *Under the Sun*, *Faith*, *The Memoirs of Sherlock Holmes*, *Adam Bede* and *Chaucer*. She most recently guest-starred in the third season of *Grantchester*. Film credits include *A Caribbean Dream*, *Trance*, *Burke and Wills*, *White Mischief* and *A Dry White Season*.

LAURA MORGAN – Lola

Laura graduated from RADA in 2011. Since then she has appeared in *Prisoners'*
Wives (BBC); *The Suspicions of Mr Whicher* (ITV); *Lucky Man* (Sky 1);
Dark Angel (ITV). Laura also played Joan of Arc in *The Hollow Crown* (BBC).
Theatre work includes *Deposit* (Hampstead Theatre); Portia in *The Merchant of*
Venice and the Wife of Bath in *The Canterbury Tales* (Cunard QM2, The RADA
Studios and Hampton Court); *Love & Money* (RADA Festival). Laura also
records audiobooks for RNIB, and continuity for 4music and The Box
music channels.

Meet the Creative Team

HOWARD BRENTON – Playwright

Howard Brenton was born in 1942. He has written over fifty plays. The most recent are *Paul* (National Theatre, 2005); *In Extremis* (Shakespeare's Globe, 2006/7; toured in 2013 retitled *Eternal Love*); *Never So Good* (National Theatre 2008); *Anne Boleyn* (Shakespeare's Globe, 2010, revived there 2011 and toured in 2013; winner of the Whatsonstage Best Play Award and UK Theatre Awards Best Touring Production); *55 Days* (Hampstead Theatre, 2012); *#aiww: The Arrest of Ai Weiwei* (Hampstead, 2013); *The Guffin* (one-act play, NT Connections, 2013); *Drawing the Line* (Hampstead Theatre, 2013); *Doctor Scroggy's War* (Shakespeare's Globe, 2014); *Ransomed* (one-act play, Salisbury Playhouse, 2015); *Lawrence After Arabia* (Hampstead Theatre, 2016) and *The Blinding Light* (Jermyn Street Theatre 2017).

Versions of classics include *The Life of Galileo* (National Theatre, 1980; *Danton's Death* (National Theatre, 1982, and a new version in 2010) and Goethe's *Faust* (RSC, 1995/6.) He adapted Robert Tressell's *The Ragged Trousered Philanthropists* (Liverpool Everyman and Chichester Festival Theatre, 2010. *Dances of Death* (after Strindberg) was presented by the Gate Theatre, Notting Hill in 2013. His version of Strindberg's *Miss Julie* is playing at the Theatre by the Lake, Keswick, and will come to Jermyn Street Theatre in November.

TOM LITTLER – Director

Tom is the new Artistic Director of Jermyn Street Theatre. He was Artistic Director of Primavera for over ten years, Associate Director of Theatre503, and Associate Director of the Peter Hall Company. Other collaborations with Howard Brenton include the premieres of Brenton's versions of *Miss Julie* (Theatre by the Lake and Jermyn Street Theatre) and *Dances of Death* (Gate Theatre), and a revival of *Bloody Poetry* (Jermyn Street Theatre). Tom has directed over fifty plays and musicals in London, the UK, and Europe, including *Good Grief* with Penelope Keith (Theatre Royal Bath and national tour); *The Picture of Dorian Gray*, *The Glass Menagerie* (English Theatre, Frankfurt); *A Little Night Music* (Budapest); *First Episode*, *The Living Room* (Jermyn Street Theatre); *Saturday Night* (West End); *Measure for Measure* (Cambridge Arts Theatre); *Much Ado About Nothing*, *Twelfth Night* (Guildford Shakespeare Company); *Merit*, *Jingo* (Finborough Theatre); *As You Like It* (Creation Theatre); *Murder in the Cathedral* (Oxford Playhouse/Christ Church Cathedral); *Absurd Person Singular* (national tour). He trained as an Assistant/Associate Director to leading figures including Alan Strachan, Peter Gill, Sir Peter Hall and Sir Trevor Nunn. His productions have been nominated for numerous Critics' Choice and Off West End Awards. Tom lives in Cambridge, where he does some research and teaching of English Literature at Cambridge University.

CHERRY TRULUCK for Lucky Bert – Set Designer

Cherry's award-nominated theatre design work stretches back to 2004 with over 40 shows in the UK & internationally, including *All That Fall* (Jermyn Street Theatre, Arts Theatre and 59E59 New York); *Religion and Anarchy, The Living Room* (Jermyn Street Theatre); *Martine* (Finborough). Lucky Bert are a live art and performance design collective led by Cherry Truluck and Alberta Jones. Recent Lucky Bert designs include *Testosterone* (Rhum & Clay/British Council Showcase/Pleasance Theatre/tour); *Chess* (Canterbury Christchurch University); *Intergalactic Caravan* (festival tour); *Post* (Xavier De Sousa, Ovalhouse); *I Have Been Here Before* (Jermyn Street Theatre). Live Art includes *Complex States* (Group Exhibition, Waseda University Tokyo); *It's All Going to the Dogs* (performance installation, Strangelove Festival); *ReACT: When Live Art Met Brexit* (site-specific installation & festival, Red Door Studios). Upcoming: *The Masters of Mystery* (Marlowe Studio) and Lucky Bert's own programme of work for the Folkestone Triennial, The Architecture of Anxiety. Cherry is also an assistant professor for MFA Global Art Practice, Central Saint Martins/Tokyo University of the Arts and Lucky Bert have run performance and design workshops for Arts Depot and Roundhouse London among many others.

MAX PAPPENHEIM – Composer & Sound Designer

Theatre includes *Miss Julie* (Theatre by the Lake/Jermyn Street Theatre); *The Children* (Royal Court/Broadway); *Sex with Strangers, Labyrinth* (Hampstead Theatre); *Ophelias Zimmer* (Schaubühne, Berlin/Royal Court); *A Fox on the Fairway* (Queen's Theatre, Hornchurch); *The Lottery of Love, Sheppey, Blue/Heart, Little Light, The Distance* (Orange Tree, Richmond); *The Gaul* (Hull Truck); *Toast* (national tour/59E59/Park Theatre); *Jane Wenham* (Out of Joint); *Waiting for Godot* (Sheffield Crucible); *My Eyes Went Dark* (59E59/Traverse Theatre/Finborough Theatre); *Cargo* (Arcola Theatre); *CommonWealth* (Almeida Theatre); *Creve Coeur* (Print Room); *Wink* (Theatre503); *And Here I Am, Fabric, Invincible* (national tours); *Spamalot, The Glass Menagerie* (English Theatre, Frankfurt); *The Cardinal, Kiki's Delivery Service, Johnny Got His Gun, Our Ajax* (Southwark Playhouse); *Mrs Lowry and Son* (Trafalgar Studios); *Martine, Black Jesus, Somersaults, The Fear of Breathing* (Finborough Theatre); *Shopera: Carmen* (Royal Opera House/Barbican); *The Hotel Plays* (Langham Hotel). As Associate, *The Island* (Young Vic); *Fleabag* (Soho Theatre). Associate Artist of The Faction and of Silent Opera. Radio includes *Home Front* (BBC Radio 4).

WILLIAM REYNOLDS – Lighting Designer
Previously at Jermyn Street Theatre, William designed set and lighting
for *Saturday Night* (also West End) and set for *Bloody Poetry*. His other recent
set and lighting designs include *Jungle Book* (London Wonderground and
international tour); *Rites of War*, *Blown Away* (UK tour); *Radiant
Vermin* (Soho Theatre and Brits Off Broadway); *Tonight With Donny
Stixx*, *Dark Vanilla Jungle*, *Tender Napalm* (Soho Theatre and UK tour); *Arab
Nights* (Soho Theatre and UK tour); *Daredevas* (Southbank
Centre). Projection designs include *Prima Donna* (Sadler's Wells); *The
Gambler* (Royal Opera House) and *Home* (Theatre Royal Bath). William is
also Artistic Director of Metta Theatre www.mettatheatre.co.uk.

EMILY STUART – Costume Designer
Emily Stuart trained at Wimbledon School of Art. Costume-design credits
include *Bloody Poetry*, *Anyone Can Whistle*, *Natural Affection*, *The Living
Room* (Jermyn Street Theatre); *Much Ado About Nothing* (Shakespeare in the
Squares); *Robinson Crusoe*, *Robin Hood* (The Theatre, Chipping Norton);
Martine (Finborough Theatre); *Shiverman (*Theatre503); *Antigone*, *The Fifth
Column*, *What the Women Did* (Southwark Playhouse); *Murder In The
Cathedral* (Oxford Playhouse); *London Wall* (Finborough Theatre/St James
Theatre); *Flock* (Northern Stage); *Lingua France* (Finborough Theatre/59E59
New York); *EX* (Soho Theatre). Emily has twice been the recipient of the Off
West End Award for Best Costume Design for *Anyone Can Whistle* (2011) and
The Cutting of the Cloth (2016). She was nominated in the same category in
2014 for *Martine*. Film credits include *Drunken Butterflies* (Rockhopper
Productions) and *London Wall* (Master Media). She has recently been
working on film installations with the Postal Museum (opening 2017) and
The SS Great Britain (opening 2018).

STELLA POWELL-JONES – Associate Director
Stella Powell-Jones is Deputy Director at Jermyn Street Theatre. Recent work
in the UK includes *This Is Our Youth* (Platform Presents); as Associate, Caryl
Churchill's *Escaped Alone* (Royal Court/international tour); Florian
Zeller's *The Father* (West End/national tour) and access work with EXTANT –
Britain's leading professional performing-arts company of visually impaired
people. In the US, recent credits include the world premiere of Samuel D.
Hunter's *The Healing* (Theatre Breaking Through Boundaries, NYC); the West
Coast premiere of Nick Jones's *Trevor* (Circle X Theatre); and Bathsheba
Doran's *The Mystery of Love and Sex* (Signature Theatre). Also in the US,
Stella has developed new work with the Kennedy Center, the Huntington
Theatre and Playwrights Horizons, amongst others.

Production Credits

Associate Set Designer	Alberta Jones for Lucky Bert
Stage Manager	Rachel Reeve
Set Builder	Hugo Sterk for Sterk Studio
Production Electrician	Thom Collins
Costume Assistant	Lucy Cronin
Costume Maker	Laura Le Bayon
Costume Hires	COSPROP
Assistant to Set Designer	Jemima Owen
Rehearsal Space	Jerwood Space

Rehearsal Photography	Gennie Allcott
Production Photography	Robert Workman
Public Relations	David Burns
Graphic Design	Visual Things

Produced and General Managed by Jermyn Street Theatre

With special thanks to all those who offer financial support to enable Jermyn Street Theatre to produce our work, and to all at the Jerwood Space.

SUBSIDISED REHEARSAL FACILITIES PROVIDED BY

JERWOOD SPACE

JERMYN STREET THEATRE

During the 1930s, the basement of 16b Jermyn Street – close to Piccadilly in the heart of London's West End – was home to the glamorous Monseigneur Restaurant and Club. The space was converted into a theatre by Howard Jameson and Penny Horner in the early 1990s and Jermyn Street Theatre staged its first production in August 1994. The theatre director Neil Marcus became the first Artistic Director in 1995 and secured Lottery funding for the venue; the producer Chris Grady also made a major contribution to the theatre's development. In the late 1990s, the Artistic Director was David Babani, later the founder and Artistic Director of the Menier Chocolate Factory.

Over the last twenty years the theatre has established itself as one of London's leading Off-West End studio theatres, with hit productions including *Barefoot in the Park* with Alan Cox and Rachel Pickup, directed by Sally Hughes, and *Helping Harry* with Adrian Lukis and Simon Dutton, directed by Nickolas Grace. Gene David Kirk, accompanied by Associate Director Anthony Biggs, became Artistic Director in the late 2000s and reshaped the theatre's creative output with revivals of rarely performed plays, including Charles Morgan's post-war classic *The River Line*, the UK premiere of Ibsen's first performed play *St John's Night*, and another Ibsen, *Little Eyolf* starring Imogen Stubbs and Doreen Mantle. Tom Littler staged two acclaimed Stephen Sondheim revivals: *Anyone Can Whistle*, starring Issy van Randwyck and Rosalie Craig, and *Saturday Night*, which transferred to the Arts Theatre.

In 2012 Trevor Nunn directed the world premiere of Samuel Beckett's radio play *All That Fall* starring Eileen Atkins and Michael Gambon. The production subsequently transferred to the Arts Theatre and then to New York's 59E59 Theatre. Jermyn Street Theatre was nominated for the Peter Brook Empty Space Award in 2011 and won The Stage 100 Best Fringe Theatre in 2012.

Anthony Biggs became Artistic Director in 2013, combining his love of rediscoveries with a new focus on emerging artists and writers from outside the UK. Recent revivals include Eugene O'Neill's early American work *The First Man*, Terence Rattigan's first play *First Episode*, John Van Druten's First World War drama *Flowers of the Forest*, and a repertory season of South African drama. New work includes US playwright Ruby Rae Spiegel's *Dry Land*, Jonathan Lewis's *A Level Playing Field*, and Sarah Daniels' *Soldiers' Wives* starring Cath Shipton.

This summer, Anthony Biggs stepped down and Tom Littler took over as Artistic Director. Littler has previously been Associate Director of new-writing venue Theatre503 and Associate Director of the Peter Hall Company. He founded the theatre company Primavera and ran it for over ten years, winning numerous awards. His opening production, the world premiere of Howard Brenton's *The Blinding Light*, is his sixth at Jermyn Street Theatre.

Throughout its history, the theatre's founders, Howard Jameson and Penny Horner, have continued to serve as Chair of the Board and Executive Director respectively, and the generous donors, front of house staff, and tireless volunteers all play their parts in the Jermyn Street Theatre story.

Arthouse Theatre in the Heart of the West End

Tom Littler is relaunching Jermyn Street Theatre as a full-scale producing theatre, creating around eight to ten productions every year. Littler's vision for Jermyn Street Theatre is to create a thriving hub for arthouse theatre in the heart of the West End. The priorities are the staging of outstanding new plays, rare revivals, new versions of European classics, and high-quality musicals, alongside one-off literary events. Through a major fundraising campaign, and co-productions with prestigious venues and companies throughout the UK and Europe, Jermyn Street Theatre will spread its work further afield, and become an intimate home for entertaining, intelligent drama.

Meet the Team

Honorary Patron
HRH Princess Michael of Kent

Chair of the Board
Howard Jameson

***

Artistic Director
Tom Littler

Executive Director
Penny Horner

Deputy Director Stella Powell-Jones*	**Duty Managers** Martin Ayres Adam Ishaq
Resident Producer Julia Mucko**	Laura Jury-Hyde Pam Keen
Artistic Associate Natasha Rickman	Sarah Lark Adam Lilley Grace Wessels
Trainee Director (Birkbeck College) Tom McClane-Williamson	**Bar Team** Mandy Berger
Technical Manager Thom Collins	Jerry Cox Wendy Ann Jefferies
Building Manager Jon Wadey	**Technicians** David Harvey
Public Relations David Burns PR	Steve Lowe

*The Deputy Director position is sponsored by the Carne Trust.

**The Resident Producer position is sponsored by an anonymous private donor, and mentored by Rachael Williams.

Find us at
www.jermynstreettheatre.co.uk
@JSTheatre
Box Office: 020 7287 2875
16b Jermyn Street, London SW1Y 6ST

The Self-Experimenter

I wrote *The Blinding Light* to try to understand the mental and spiritual crisis that August Strindberg suffered in February, 1896. Deeply disturbed, plagued by hallucinations, he holed up in various hotel rooms in Paris, most famously in the Hotel Orfila in the Rue d'Assas.

He'd had great success in Paris. A revival of *Miss Julie* in 1893 created a sensation and, in 1895, *The Father* had been rapturously received. But now he abandoned playwriting. He announced he was not a writer but a true 'natural scientist', an alchemist. His hands burnt by chemicals, he attempted to make gold.

He chronicled the experience in his novel *Inferno*. Like so much of his autobiographical writing, it is unreliable. Truth in Strindberg is, shall we say, a moveable reality – as he says in my play, 'The bright memories are always true.' But it is beyond doubt that he was in the midst of a psychotic episode, dedicated to alchemy and convinced supernatural forces were trying to stop his experiments. The Strindberg scholar Michael Robinson told me that, in the 1970s, researching in the Royal Library in Stockholm, he opened a notebook of Strindberg's never looked at before – the huge archive was then not fully explored. Small strips of card, two inches long, fell out. At their ends they had a yellowy stain. They were for testing for gold.

But there is another way of looking at what some see as a total breakdown. He had taken the realism of plays like *The Father*, *Creditors* and *Miss Julie*, in its day an extreme and revolutionary theatre, as far as he could. He'd hit a wall. Strindberg wrote and lived off his instincts, his feelings, swinging between extremes; he's been called one of the first modernists, but he was also one of the last romantics. Instinctively, despite the psychosis and the absinthe, he was trying to destroy then rebuild his view of the world. He was experimenting on himself.

And alchemy was an ideal guide. Like all mystic systems it is a process of steps towards perfection. First everything must be broken down in the stage of 'putrefaction'. Only then can the ascent to the final stage begin, 'coagulation': the transformation of all that is base into incorruptible gold. But – and this greatly appealed to Strindberg – to achieve the chemical process the alchemist must, in parallel, break down his own very being to be able to ascend to a final state of realisation. Alchemy is a moral quest.

Bonkers? But it worked. After four years' silence, Strindberg returned to the theatre with a series of fantastical plays such as *A Dream Play*, *The Ghost Sonata* and *To Damascus*. Were the alchemy and the playwriting actually part of the same project? Before and after the crisis in Paris he always wanted to make the theatre *more real*, at first by being true to the minutiae of everyday life – the famous cooking on stage in *Miss Julie* – then by trying to stage psychological states so vividly you think you are dreaming wide awake. By 'realist' or 'expressionist' means he wanted audiences to see the world in a new light.

Howard Brenton
August 2017

THE BLINDING LIGHT

Howard Brenton

Characters

AUGUST
LOLA, *a hotel cleaner*
SIRI, *August's first wife*
FRIDA, *August's second wife*

The play is set in February 1896 in the Hotel Orfila,
Rue d'Assas, Paris

*This text went to press before the end of rehearsals and so may
differ slightly from the play as performed.*

Scene One

February 1896. A squalid top-floor room in the Hotel Orfila, Rue d'Assas, Paris.

AUGUST, *hands red.*

LOLA, *maid and cleaner at the Orfila. She has a mop and a bucket.*

LOLA. I'm a cleaner, I clean, that's what I do.

She makes a move, he blocks her.

I've got to do the bathroom, monsieur!

AUGUST. You're not doing the bathroom!

LOLA. Don't give me grief. I just got this job. It's shitty work but I need it.

AUGUST. Why does the management suddenly want to clean in here? They never have before.

LOLA. That I can see. What's the yellow stain?

AUGUST. A failed oxidisation.

LOLA. Sounds kind of kinky.

AUGUST. I – I've paid for these rooms. What I do in them is my inalienable right!

LOLA. Your what?

AUGUST. I know the creatures of the passing show, the wise who think me mad, would sneer. But this is my kingdom! This is where I will open the door to the hidden world!

LOLA. What door's that?

AUGUST. It's mystic.

LOLA. Misty?

AUGUST. Mystical! In the mind! In the head! In – another dimension! Leading to the future!

LOLA. I don't want to open no door to the future, I want to open the door to your bathroom.

An exasperated gesture by AUGUST. LOLA *reads it as aggressive.*

You wanta hit me? Word of advice – don't wanta hit me. I know how to deal with men who wanta hit me.

AUGUST. You are violating a reality you cannot perceive.

LOLA. Yeah. Right.

She opens the bathroom door, about to step in.

AUGUST. Hermes Trismegistus, come to my aid.

But LOLA *recoils and slams the door shut, mop and bucket flung away. She retches.*

LOLA. Fucking bloody Ada, what's in the bath?

AUGUST. It's not a bomb.

LOLA. That horrible stuff! And all them tubes!

AUGUST. I am not a terrorist! I am not making a bomb!

They are looking at each other. LOLA *is breathless.*

LOLA. I gotta tell the management.

She moves.

AUGUST. It's gold.

She stops.

LOLA. What do you mean, gold?

AUGUST. I practise alchemy, a science, the true science.

LOLA. That in there's not gold, it's a – stinky sludge, and it's – sort of black!

AUGUST. It's a work-in-progress.

LOLA. The police have told the hotels – look out for oddballs. Cos of the bombings. And if you're not an oddball I don't know who is.

AUGUST. We're all odd. We're human.

LOLA. I think you're dangerous.

AUGUST. Course I am, I'm a man.

She looks at him then laughs.

LOLA. What a what a stupid, pathetic, weedy thing to say.

AUGUST. Weedy?

LOLA. Are you a drunk?

AUGUST. Alcohol's – an occupational hazard.

LOLA. Is it now. Well, being pissed in Paris is nothing special. Nah you're not dangerous, you're just a weedy drunk.

AUGUST. A stupid, pathetic, weedy drunk.

LOLA. You've got lovely blue eyes but I can see it in 'em.

AUGUST. See what?

LOLA. The pit of hell.

AUGUST. You're very forthright.

LOLA. That's just me.

AUGUST. I am dangerous, because if I make gold life will change for ever.

LOLA. Going to be rich, are you?

AUGUST. All of humanity will be rich.

LOLA. And how do you make that out?

AUGUST. Because the old science won't work. We must re-pattern reality. Humanity will have to think of the world in a new way.

LOLA *blows a raspberry.*

What?

LOLA. You talk like one more dreggy, druggy poet.

AUGUST. I am not a poet, I've given all that up –

LOLA. I see loads of you in the cafés, sounding off about 'the world'. When all you're really after is a fuck.

AUGUST. Don't be vulgar.

LOLA. Ooh, dear oh dear –

AUGUST. I hate vulgarity. It diminishes the soul.

LOLA. Poor you.

AUGUST. I've been branded vulgar! Branded by the unseen powers!

He points to his forehead.

That's where they did it. To make me the man with the mark.

LOLA. Let me see.

She closes on him and looks at his forehead.

There's nothing there. I do like the eyes, though.

He backs away sharply. She laughs.

So sensitive! Yeah, a poet if I ever saw one.

AUGUST. I'm a scientist! A true scientist, an alchemist.

A pause.

LOLA. So – how much?

AUGUST. How much for what?

LOLA. How much'll you pay me? For not letting on about the mess all this science makes in your bathroom?

AUGUST. I am – a bit stretched.

LOLA. Are you now? Right, management, police –

AUGUST. I'll give you some gold.

LOLA. You mean you've actually made it?

AUGUST. Theoretically.

LOLA. You have made gold in your bath? Out of that muck?

AUGUST. In theory.

LOLA. What's that mean?

AUGUST. The transformation is there. It's just – veiled. I need more time.

LOLA. Ha! Everyone in hotels like this says that. Give me more time and I'll pay the rent. More time and I'll stop drinking, be rich, save my marriage, start a revolution, turn into a bird and fly away through the window. Sorry, monsieur –

She turns to go.

AUGUST. Did they send you?

LOLA. Did who send me?

A distortion begins.

Then AUGUST *speaks to her, not aside. She is blank.*

AUGUST. You're not a cleaner. You're one of them, aren't you?

They are staring at each other.

A silence.

Speak to me.

A silence.

The management didn't send you, this dump is never cleaned. You're from another power!

A silence.

Silence. Yes. That's right. Words conceal, but silence hides nothing. How did language begin? To keep tribal secrets. Language is all cyphers, you need a key. But silence – you need no key. You stare into it. And the mask is torn from the deceiver's face. (*A beat.*) I'll go into the silence.

A silence. She is still blank.

You've hunted me in the streets, you've sent signs crowding in on me, everything meaning everything else, desperate for it to be six-fifteen in the evening, absinthe time – I – but here in my room, I've got to be safe, I must be –

LOLA. Safe? (*Laughs.*) Of course you're not. Don't you know we can go anywhere? You think your craft is strong enough to keep us out? Don't you know we can come through the walls, like a gas, into your lungs, and your blood, and your mind? (*A beautiful smile.*) We have a choice – we can choke you, or send you mad.

AUGUST. What do you want –

LOLA. To warn you. Stop your experiments.

The distortion stops abruptly. LOLA *and* AUGUST *again.*

Did who send me?

He stares at her for a moment then collects himself.

AUGUST. No one. No.

LOLA. Looks like it's absinthe time for you.

AUGUST. I'm not drinking. It's day twenty-nine.

LOLA. Ha! Day counting, are you? My father got to thirty-one once. Usually it was three or four. Then it was zero every day, all day long – till the bastard fell down the stairwell and smashed his head open.

They are looking at each other, warily.

So, what, you been doing this alchemistry stuff twenty-nine days?

AUGUST. Three months.

LOLA. Three months, stuck in here?

AUGUST. It's safe. Or it has been.

LOLA. No visitors?

He looks at her.

Lady friends?

AUGUST. None of your business.

She shrugs.

LOLA. Course not, but I want to know I'm dealing with a gent. Or someone who passes for one.

He hesitates. Then –

AUGUST. My ex-wife's been in Paris, but we've not been seeing each other. And now she's in Berlin. Actually I – steeled myself to see her off yesterday, at the Gare de l'Est.

LOLA. Very gentlemanly. Chucked you for a Kraut, did she?

AUGUST. That is too forward!

LOLA. Don't get uppity, we all live the same stories.

A pause.

So. Solitary animal?

AUGUST. I have renounced human contact.

LOLA. No sex?

AUGUST. That is beyond forward.

LOLA. Ooh ooh, back and forward, back and forward. Tell you what – I'll give you a week.

AUGUST. A –

LOLA. Make me some gold in a week from now, then I won't let on to the manager.

AUGUST. How much do you want?

LOLA. A couple of kilos?

AUGUST *laughs.*

AUGUST. Maybe enough for a ring.

LOLA. Why would I want a ring?

AUGUST. You can pawn it.

LOLA. Coo! For a moment there I thought you wanted to marry me.

AUGUST. I told you, I have renounced. I've had enough of
   marriages.

LOLA. ' –es'? How many?

He's reluctant to say.

AUGUST. Just the two.

LOLA. Oh, so you were seeing number two off on the train!
   Well. Two wives, what, couldn't they stand what you got up
   to in the bath? Or bed?

AUGUST. You are totally inappropriate!

LOLA. Yeah? That good or bad?

A sexual flash between them.

   I better get on. They said start at the top so you're the first
   guest I've done. If the rest are like you I dunno what I'll do.

AUGUST. But my secret's safe. The alchemy.

LOLA. If I get my ring next week.

She turns to go.

AUGUST. Are you at least going to clean in here?

LOLA. You've got to be joking.

She goes to leave, with a clatter of mop and bucket.

AUGUST. You're not real, are you.

LOLA. Not real? Hunh! Sometimes I wish I weren't.

AUGUST. The Orfila doesn't allow women.

LOLA. No women? Do you know what goes on in the rooms all
   the way down, under this garret of yours?

AUGUST. The Orfila is run by monks!

LOLA. Monks? Pimps more like.

AUGUST. You're not real. If I clap my hands you'll disappear.

He claps his hands. She stares at him.

LOLA. Right. See you next Tuesday. If you've got my gold
ring, maybe I'll do you. The room I mean. (*Laughs*.) Bye
bye, blue eyes.

She exits with a clatter of cleaning things.

AUGUST *sinks down, his back against the wall.*

AUGUST. I have always played the seduced, not the seducer.

I know I do that. Even as I'm doing it. Know thyself, but you
do, and it's no help at all.

The woman who was just here, did I flirt with her, did she
with me? Can a man and woman meet, even if total
strangers, and not, in seconds, have the hooks in each other,
pulling back and forth, like a terrible magnetism of the flesh?

How I loved it, though. I played with life until it smashed me
to the ground.

'Oh dear, poor you, see yourself as some kind of hero?'

Arms against a sea...

'Come off it, August, you're no Hamlet, you're just a sad
little man in a smelly room talking to himself.'

Don't disguise yourself as me.

'But I am you. In every detail.'

He pauses, dead still, eyes flickering.

Where are you?

'Where are you?'

You're next door!

'YOU'RE next door.'

*He stumbles to a wall, crouches, puts his ear to it. He moves
along the wall. He stands, goes to the centre of the room,
stamps, whirls round as if he has heard a sound next door.
He stamps twice.*

Everything I do in this room, you do.

'Everything I do in THIS room, you do.'

He leans cheek against the wall, running his hand over it.

You're there, aren't you.

He moves his hand over the wall.

You're moving your hand – there! There! No!

He stands.

I have demonstrated the presence of carbon in sulphur. I hold on to that.

He goes to a floorboard. It's loose. He takes it up. A bottle of absinthe is concealed there. It is two-thirds full, with a stopper. He raises it.

Death to poetry, long live science!

He swigs.

At once intense light.

Blackout.

Lights up. By a stage trick the bottle lies empty on the floor. AUGUST is slumped against the wall.

Day one.

A blackout.

In the dark, whispers.

Scene Two

Lights up. The whispers stop.

Enter LOLA. *She does not have the cleaning things with her. She sees him slumped against the wall.*

LOLA. Oh no.

AUGUST *panics.*

AUGUST. Is it Tuesday?

LOLA. What, think you've lost a week?

AUGUST. Days – fold in.

LOLA. You really are in a bad way.

AUGUST. Fold in, on themselves. It's happened to me before.

LOLA. You talking about blacking out?

AUGUST. An out-of-the-world experience.

LOLA. Yup, blacking out.

She takes a step.

AUGUST. Stand still!

LOLA. What –

AUGUST. You're in the beam.

LOLA. The –

AUGUST. Is that necklace metal?

LOLA. The bloke who gave it me said it were platinum, but I
    guess it's the usual trash –

AUGUST. Thank God it's not platinum, that would be very bad.

LOLA. Why?

AUGUST. Connectivity.

LOLA. I don't know what you –

She makes to move.

AUGUST. Don't – the current will kill you!

She stops. He approaches her carefully as he explains, ducking beneath an invisible beam.

It's electricity. It comes in pulses, that wall to that wall, into my bedroom. They're trying to electrocute me. Fortunately my bed is brass which, of course, is a bad conductor. I only get low shocks.

LOLA. I don't feel a thing –

AUGUST. But a pulse is coming. Can't you hear the machine?

LOLA. Not really –

AUGUST. Let me –

He is behind her. He unclasps the necklace.

LOLA. No fondling –

He removes the necklace.

AUGUST. Step away! Now!

She steps away quickly.

AUGUST *yells and throws the necklace to the floor as if it's hot, rubbing his hands.*

Just in time.

They look at the necklace on the floor. Then LOLA *picks it up. She holds it out to show it is not hot.*

LOLA. I think you've got problems.

AUGUST. I do, legions of problems, all kinds of forces are out to get me.

A beat.

LOLA. Yeah. Look, I just popped up to tell you there are women in the café who say they know you.

AUGUST. Women?

LOLA. In the café opposite.

AUGUST. How many women?

LOLA. How many do you want? Tables of us, laughing at you?

AUGUST. They're laughing at me?

LOLA. Don't worry, there're only two of 'em.

AUGUST. Are they laughing about – intimate details?

LOLA. Well, they are those ex-wives of yours.

A beat.

AUGUST. That's not possible.

LOLA. That's who they say they are.

AUGUST. They couldn't bear to be in the same room together, let alone sit at a café table!

LOLA. But there they are, ganging up against you.

AUGUST. No. Frida's in Berlin. And Siri has no idea I'm in Paris. (*A beat.*) Does she? I wrote to the children. Yes. I put the address of the hotel at the top, I was desperate to hear back from them, I should have just written 'Paris, February' – but there's always the drive to be specific. Date, time, place, detail – dress, accent, the pattern of plates on a dresser. I've always yearned to make things be real, to hold on to –

LOLA *laughs*.

What's funny?

LOLA. One of 'em said you'd be discombobulated.

AUGUST. Discom– one of Frida's words.

LOLA. Anyway, they gave me a couple of francs and asked if you were here.

AUGUST. And you betrayed me.

LOLA. I don't even know you, mister. Can't betray someone you don't know, can you?

AUGUST. Easily. Look, say to them I'm not here, I've gone to – Skovlyst.

LOLA. Where?

AUGUST. Siri will understand.

LOLA *thinks about it*.

LOLA. No, can't do that.

AUGUST. Remember the ring.

LOLA. I don't believe in that for a second.

AUGUST. Yes, you do. The more imaginary the gold, the more we believe in it.

A blackout.

Whispers. And…

Scene Three

SIRI *and* AUGUST.

A silence.

SIRI. You've been writing to the children.

AUGUST. Yes, that's it! I knew that's how you'd sniff me out. Like a bloodhound bitch, following the artist's scent all the way to Paris.

SIRI. Dear God, August, how far gone are you?

A wave of his hand.

AUGUST. Way out the other side. Sh. Sh. The machine's stopped.

SIRI. Machine?

AUGUST. He's moved it up into the loft. To direct the beam down through the ceiling. But he's having technical problems.

SIRI. What are you talking about?

AUGUST. Oh, it's nothing, nothing, you know – hotel living, annoying guests in other rooms. (*A beat.*) What were you doing in the café with Frida?

SIRI. Café?

AUGUST. You and Frida were in the café across the street.

SIRI. I've never met that woman in my life and if I did I – don't think I could control myself.

AUGUST. You were sitting there with her, laughing about me!

SIRI. Who told you this nonsense?

AUGUST. The cleaning woman saw you.

SIRI. What cleaning woman?

AUGUST. She saw you, my two ex-wives, conspiring together!

SIRI. August, I was never in the café –

AUGUST. No! She saw you!

SIRI. Stop this. Just stop it. Or I'll have to –

AUGUST. Have to what?

SIRI. Never mind.

AUGUST. No, what?

SIRI. Intervene.

AUGUST. Intervene? How?

SIRI. I've talked to doctors.

AUGUST. So! The two of you in the café – you were plotting, what, a medical intervention?

SIRI. Would you like it if we had been?

AUGUST. What did you say to Frida?

SIRI. I told you, I was not in some café with that tart, that homebreaker!

AUGUST. How – how dare you talk to doctors about me!

SIRI. August, of course I spoke to someone, I'm scared for you, all the occult nonsense. So please, reassure me, just – talk about something normal, something real.

A pause.

AUGUST. What normal, real thing comes to mind?

She shrugs.

SIRI. The smell? Is it from the bathroom? Have you killed something in there?

AUGUST. Just The Enlightenment.

SIRI. How – I mean – how can you live like this?

AUGUST. It's not easy, squalor takes a lot of thought and practice, neglecting oneself is as exhausting as good hygiene.

SIRI. I used to find you exotic.

AUGUST. I used to find you exotic.

SIRI. The debauched, 'the world is all against me' artist.

AUGUST. The snobby, 'treading on roses all the way', upper-class little girl lost.

SIRI. What were we thinking of?

AUGUST. I haven't the faintest idea.

SIRI. Nor do I.

A pause.

AUGUST. You appear out of thin air and threaten me with doctors. Why, what do you want?

SIRI. You know what I want.

A pause.

AUGUST. Actually, you loved the madness.

SIRI. And you loved fucking an aristocrat.

AUGUST. I rescued you from that world!

SIRI. Stole me from my husband, you mean.

AUGUST. It wasn't like that and you know it.

SIRI. So what was it like? Me, young, married to a rich man? And then I see you – destitute, working for pennies as a librarian. And I fall?

AUGUST. Did you not? Lowered yourself! Always dangerous, always with consequences. In love affairs, finally a creditor comes knocking on the door. Lovers see his black hand between theirs as they eat at their table, they hear his harsh breathing in the stillness of the night, they try to flee from a memory that dogs them, a debt they've not paid, and because they're not strong enough to carry the burden of their guilt they turn upon each other.

SIRI. You – miserable, mean, scribbler of a man. You're quoting from that play you put me in.

AUGUST. It wasn't you.

SIRI. I was Laura in *The Father*.

AUGUST. She's – the reality transformed.

SIRI. It was cringingly, horribly clear to everyone 'the reality' was me!

AUGUST. It was art!

SIRI. Art? Oh phooey.

AUGUST. It was – distorted, written in anger, plays should always be written in anger. (*A beat.*) Anyway I was – quoting *Creditors*, not *The Father*.

SIRI. Whoops, naughty little ex-wifey, doesn't know ex-hubby's work backwards. Tekla in *Creditors*, yes. Are all the vicious bitches in your plays meant to be me? You threw a lamp at me, remember? And what does your surrogate do in *The Father*? Throw a lamp at his wife.

AUGUST. How many times – the Captain in *The Father* is not me, and Laura is not you. Everything is transmuted –

SIRI. Can you imagine what it was like, to sit there, watching that scene?

AUGUST. But you never saw *The Father.*

SIRI. I sneaked in, to witness my humiliation.

AUGUST. It's the Captain who is humiliated!

SIRI. You don't understand your own work at all, do you?

AUGUST. It's about transformation! I want things on the stage to be so real that lives in the audience are changed!

SIRI. Oh, your plays changed lives. I speak from bitter experience. (*A beat.*) I could have shot you.

AUGUST. That would have been – a solution.

SIRI. There was a moment, actually.

AUGUST. What moment?

SIRI. Oh –

AUGUST. No, what moment?

SIRI. At Skovlyst.

AUGUST. In the garden.

SIRI. Yes, that garden –

A distortion begins.

Everything overgrown.

AUGUST. A rotting smell, old leaves. I'm in dark shade. Walking toward the sunlight on the lake. But something makes me turn – and you're standing in the doorway of the summerhouse.

SIRI. Am I?

AUGUST. With the gun pointing at me.

SIRI. What gun?

AUGUST. Ludwig's pistol.

Out of the distortion.

He used it to shoot squirrels.

SIRI. Don't be ridiculous. I never pointed a pistol at you!
(*Low*.) Though God knows I –

Back in the distortion.

AUGUST. You came out of the summer house, finger on the
trigger, the barrel pointed at my head!

SIRI. I don't even know there is a gun in the summer house.

AUGUST. It was on the table. I put it up on the shelf, I was
worried the children would find it.

SIRI. Gun. Summer house. Me.

Out of the distortion.

AUGUST. I thought you were playing a game. As if you were
in some ridiculous play by Ibsen.

SIRI. Gun summer house me, and hey presto, you've a scene in
your head! And you believe it.

AUGUST. The bright memories are always true.

SIRI. Ha! (*A beat*.) All right.

Back in the distortion.

All right. I take the gun down from the shelf. I load it. And
point it at your back. But you don't turn, you don't see me
about to kill you.

Out of the distortion.

AUGUST. I knew it!

SIRI. Did you, now.

They stare at each other.

AUGUST. Why didn't you pull the trigger?

SIRI. You tell me.

AUGUST. A failure of nerve.

SIRI. That would be it.

AUGUST. I never had the nerve either.

SIRI. Don't let this slide into your suicide thingy, you're at your
   worst when you're in that –

He laughs.

AUGUST. It's funny, though.

SIRI. What is?

AUGUST. That we've both failed to get rid of me.

SIRI. A choice bit of self-pity there!

AUGUST. It's not self-pity, it's an observation.

SIRI. From someone who can only see himself.

AUGUST. But I can't see myself. Sometimes I think I don't exist.

SIRI. Says the great egotist! 'I am a hole, a nothing, but a
   nothing around which all the world revolves.'

AUGUST. If you do what I do you've got to be serious about it,
   all the time!

SIRI. And if you're a mother of three children you've got to be
   serious about it, all the time – you selfish bastard!

AUGUST. You second-rate, bourgeois, talentless bitch!

SIRI. God, I wish I had shot you!

AUGUST. So do I!

   A pause.

SIRI. We're rowing.

AUGUST. Yes.

SIRI. I don't want to.

AUGUST. No.

SIRI. I can't stop.

AUGUST. Nor can I. It's hateful.

SIRI. But delicious.

   A pause.

I think I was sick when I left Carl for you. And if you say 'love is a sickness' I'll scream and go into that bathroom and smash up whatever it is you have in there.

AUGUST. Major Baron Carl Gustaf Wrangl of Sanss. Dear God, the name alone is enough to make you turn revolutionary socialist.

SIRI. Did, didn't you, for five minutes?

AUGUST. He asked you for permission to sleep with your cousin!

SIRI. If you ever put that in a play I'll –

AUGUST. You said 'yes'.

SIRI. She was in love with him and – I was in shock –

AUGUST. And you left him. And we got married.

SIRI. And I became penniless and you went bankrupt.

AUGUST. Round and round.

SIRI. Round and round.

A pause.

AUGUST. I don't know why you're here. Tell me.

SIRI. To see how you are, darling.

AUGUST. I don't believe that.

SIRI. I still have feelings for you.

AUGUST. Why do I find that sinister?

SIRI. I believe the fashionable explanation is 'paranoia'.

AUGUST. Oh, that nonsense coming out of Vienna. 'All in the mind'? No. There really are forces out to get us.

SIRI. You mean like old flames and old spouses.

AUGUST. I mean – demons.

SIRI. Demons! Is that how you see me?

AUGUST. No but demons may take your shape.

SIRI. Charming! So how do I look? Is my tail showing?

She laughs and spins.

AUGUST. Don't do that –

SIRI. What?

AUGUST. Spin. You did that, first time I saw you.

SIRI. Yes. This demon has done her research.

She smiles. Then is not smiling.

They look at each other for a moment, waiting.

AUGUST. Have you brought the children to Paris?

SIRI. Do you care?

AUGUST. How can you say that? Of course I care. Where are
they?

SIRI. They are safe. That's all you need to know.

AUGUST. It is not all I need to know! I can't – imagine them,
they're in the dark to me, it's agony not knowing what
they're doing, moment by moment, not hearing their voices,
not being able to make them laugh. Watch them sleep.

SIRI. Poor, poor you. Whether you see my children is in my gift.

AUGUST. Yes, you have that power over me.

SIRI. I do.

A pause.

You could see them if we all go back to Stockholm.

A pause.

AUGUST. Back to the cesspool? That stinking little provincial
pit writhing with snakes? The right-wing press that hates me,
Royalists who want me in jail, the left wing who think I've
sold out, petty fellow scribblers dripping poison – and as for
the feminists –

SIRI. We'll go back to Stockholm. And I'll play Miss Julie again.

AUGUST. This is what I dread –

SIRI. You think I'm not up to it?

AUGUST. You are – rather old for her now.

SIRI. Sarah Bernhardt's playing teenagers!

AUGUST. But you're not –

SIRI. Don't you dare! I am as much an artist as you! It's because of me it's your most famous play.

AUGUST. That first production was a disaster, if you recall.

SIRI. Only because the censor closed it down.

AUGUST. And when I moved the production from Stockholm to Copenhagen, because of the censor, the critics tore the play apart. Well, tore you apart.

SIRI. That was because of the stink of your reputation!

AUGUST. You slept with the leading man! And I found out!

SIRI. And rowed with him and with me. A great piece of direction, darling. You shouting and screaming at us in the wings.

AUGUST. It was in the dressing room!

SIRI. The wings! Kristin the cook was already on stage! Doing your ridiculous naturalism – frying kidneys.

AUGUST. The kidneys were revolutionary!

SIRI. You wrote Miss Julie for me. She's mine. I want to reclaim her.

A pause.

AUGUST. No. I've left the theatre. I can't bear to see the ghosts of my brain made real.

A stillness.

SIRI. If I can't get my career back, how am I to live?

AUGUST. I sent four-fifths of what I made from *The Father* here in Paris, didn't you get it?

SIRI. That was months ago.

AUGUST. Siri, accept it. I've given up playwriting. All that –
pretence. Trying to put the real on a stage.

SIRI. But you did –

AUGUST. No. I couldn't make theatre work. I couldn't use it to
find, find – (*A beat.*) So I've abandoned that world for one
far more important. True science!

SIRI. You mean the smell.

AUGUST. The smell is a by-product.

SIRI. It's the alchemy nonsense again, isn't it.

AUGUST. I am not at liberty to discuss the work.

SIRI. Why, because demons may overhear and steal it?

AUGUST. Because they may try to stop me!

SIRI. I think they may be right in Vienna, there *is* an illness of
the mind called paranoia.

AUGUST. You know, I've always sensed the other side.

SIRI. Yes, yes, 'journey to the other side', that's always what we
said when we drank together, we'll pass through this night,
this crisis, whatever it may have been, you thinking I was
sleeping with my leading man, debt, rejection by the Royal
Theatre – again – someone suing you for libel – again – the
blasphemy trial, we'll pass through it, there will be a beautiful
meadow, spring flowers amongst the grasses, birdsong, sunlit
success and happiness. But there never was that meadow.

AUGUST. There were great days, nights. There was weather for
wild strawberries.

SIRI. Oh –

She blows a rude noise.

Wild strawberries – you always got it wrong when you tried
a pretty phase. Keep to the dark and prickly, darling. Come
back to the theatre. Leave the mumbo jumbo.

AUGUST. For the mumbo jumbo of rehearsal rooms and first nights? All those false notes in the voices of people praising you, that self-aggrandisement, convincing yourself at opening parties that you have actually achieved something. When you've done nothing. Just – lied.

SIRI. It's what you do. It's what we do.

AUGUST. Let us – simply remember we had times.

SIRI. What 'times'?

AUGUST. There were broad –

SIRI. 'Broad sunlit uplands'? Are you seriously going to use that cliché about what we went through?

AUGUST. Sometimes we were at peace.

SIRI. In your head, never in mine.

AUGUST. Don't rewrite the truth.

SIRI. *You* accuse *me* of rewriting the truth?

AUGUST. We had Skovlyst.

SIRI. You've got to be joking!

AUGUST. 'Delight of the Forest', the magical castle.

SIRI. That rural slum was your Garden of Eden?

AUGUST. The strange old woman, like a crone from a fairytale, remember? She led us there. The children loved it. The woods, the strange, deserted rooms –

SIRI. And you let them run wild.

AUGUST. Children must have freedom to explore.

SIRI. Like middle-aged playwrights?

AUGUST. It was a good place for them.

SIRI. And desperately unhealthy. Mosquitoes with bites like miniature crocodiles, and rotting floorboards in the so-called castle.

AUGUST. You loved it too.

SIRI. Before you ruined it.

AUGUST. It was you who ruined it! When I found out you'd
slept with your Rochester when you were touring *Jane Eyre*.

SIRI. Actually, my Rochester was queer.

AUGUST. You had him, queer or not. Don't deny it.

SIRI. And you buggered the odd-job man in the summer house.

AUGUST. I did not –

SIRI. The summer house where I should have shot you!
I remember the disgust at the thought of his mouth on you.

AUGUST. And what of my disgust at the thought of your
mouth on other women? Anne-Marie. Are you still with
that freethinking horror? The children – you've not left them
with her –

SIRI. I told you! I'm not telling you where the children are. All
that matters is that they're safe – from you.

AUGUST. Are you saying – what – that I'm a threat to them?

SIRI. Yes.

A pause.

AUGUST. That is so cruel.

SIRI. Is it not?

AUGUST. I have always loved them.

SIRI. Oh you loved them, in a way.

AUGUST. Indulged them, I know – because –

SIRI. Because of your own unhappy childhood, brute of a father,
religious bigot of a stupid mother, the beatings, your struggle
to educate yourself, the little boy reading Shakespeare aged
eleven –

AUGUST. Seven –

SIRI. Seven, what a miracle, what a prodigy! The drama of the
dramatist's early life!

AUGUST. Don't sneer, please. Some things were real.

SIRI. Were they? So difficult to tell with you. (*A beat.*) No, you were a good father.

AUGUST. The father. (*Scoffs.*)

SIRI. There were moments.

AUGUST. There were.

SIRI. An eye in every storm.

AUGUST. Siri – Siri – none of it matters now. What happened between us went down in the flood.

SIRI. And went down in a book you wrote about our marriage.

AUGUST. Oh – that wretched book! It was an accident.

SIRI. You mean you sort of accidentally wrote a book about our marriage, in the way, say, you fall off a bar stool?

AUGUST. I never meant to publish it!

SIRI. Oh, its publication was an accident too?

AUGUST. I was told an enemy was bringing out a book about us. I couldn't allow that! You've no idea of the atmosphere in Berlin, fetid with hatred. I swear, if I could, I'd take the wretched thing back! Unpublish, burn it. But I was tricked.

SIRI. Tricked into selling it.

AUGUST. Well, I did need the money.

SIRI. It wasn't the lies, the whole twisted, slanted tackiness, it was the thought that the children would read it.

AUGUST. They can't read German, they're children.

SIRI. They may learn.

AUGUST. It's a squib.

SIRI. Full of lies about our life.

AUGUST. Minor stuff. Though it has an overriding truth.

SIRI. That you hate me.

AUGUST. I did when I wrote it. You'd just moved in with
    Anne-Marie! I daren't show my face for the mockery of it.
    Everyone was saying you and she seduced that girl of
    seventeen. And I believed it.

SIRI. Maybe we did. Does that give you the right to tell lies
    about my life?

AUGUST. I wrote what I felt.

SIRI. And what you feel is the truth?

*For a moment he hesitates, knowing he has trapped himself.
Suddenly he is exhausted.*

AUGUST. Go away, Siri, please, just leave me alone. If you are
    Siri.

SIRI. How can I, after what you wrote to Karin?

AUGUST. Oh, the letter.

SIRI. Oh, the letter.

AUGUST. Oh, that's why you're here.

SIRI. That's why I'm here, you evil man.

A pause.

AUGUST. I am the father and I am free to write to her. She's
    my child as much as yours.

SIRI. That's what scares me sick.

AUGUST. How dare you intercept my correspondence. We're
    divorced! The police state that was our marriage has been
    dissolved.

SIRI. Well, darling, I feel very much in a prison of your making.

AUGUST. I'm desperate to hear from the children. Let me,
    please. You acknowledged I was a good father.

SIRI. You did magic to make the children ill.

A pause.

You got out your spell book, or your frogs' legs or runes, wand or whatever, and cast a spell to make the children ill.

A pause.

Then you wrote to Karin, telling her what you'd done! And you sent them the spell too!

A pause.

AUGUST. It was a spell to make them feel as if they were floating, in the air, that's all! Not to make them ill! It was a joke. To amuse them. They used to love my fairytales, I wrote a book for them, it was a success, it still earns at Christmas time – it was playful, fun, I wrote it because I miss them so much, I wanted to hear from them.

SIRI. It worked.

AUGUST. What?

SIRI. Your spell worked.

AUGUST. It can't have. Did it?

SIRI. What, lost faith in your magic? A ridiculous sham after all?

AUGUST. They – floated in the air? What a triumph!

SIRI. No, they had a fever, they vomited for two days and became severely dehydrated. I had to spend money on a doctor.

AUGUST. The spell was to induce levitation. The fever had nothing to do with it.

SIRI. They made up the recipe of your disgusting potion and drank it.

AUGUST. The potion is harmless.

SIRI. It's got crushed ants in it!

AUGUST. Completely safe when boiled with vinegar.

SIRI. Enough, August! Ants in vinegar, fighting demons, alchemy, making gold in your hotel bathroom, letting yourself go, I mean look at your hands –

AUGUST. – That's the copper sulphate –

SIRI. – Babbling about 'forces', 'the other'. When you started going round public parks injecting flowers with morphine, I knew something was wrong with you.

AUGUST. That was a serious experiment to see if plants have nervous systems.

SIRI. And do they?

AUGUST. Definitely yes! They think and feel. We cannot imagine the pain of a tree being cut down.

SIRI. August – you were a rationalist, a reformer, author of a radical manifesto for women's rights, a socialist. You wanted a naturalistic theatre, made of the detail of how we actually live – I remember you lecturing me about my acting – 'be accurate, be truthful, study other people, not your own feelings, not your own fantasies'! You were the great realist! How did you come to – falling apart in a tiny room, believing any cranky idea going?

AUGUST *laughs*.

AUGUST. I am ideologically unstable? Very well, I am ideologically unstable. I contain multitudes.

SIRI. Come back to Stockholm.

AUGUST. No.

SIRI. Get back into society, the theatre.

AUGUST. No.

SIRI. All that's been between us, we'll put it aside, work together professionally.

AUGUST. No.

SIRI. It's what we're good at, if we're in this world for a reason it's to make theatre –

AUGUST. No. It's all dead.

SIRI. The children will go to a Swedish school. You'll see them every week.

AUGUST. Don't use them in this, don't!

SIRI. I need the money, August!

AUGUST. There will be money.

SIRI. When, how?

AUGUST. When I –

SIRI. When you make gold?

AUGUST. Yes. So leave me alone. I am in the midst of changing natural science! Ripping away centuries of bad theory, materialism, descending to the darkest place, to climb back to the light!

SIRI. And flog fake gold on street corners?

AUGUST. I can't speak to you. You're against the craft. You will contaminate me.

SIRI. Contam–

A pause.

I have got a certificate.

AUGUST. Oh! A certificate! What kind?

SIRI. Medical, darling.

AUGUST. And what does this medical certificate certify?

SIRI. You.

AUGUST. For what?

SIRI. Stop the experiments. Burn the occult books. Stop drinking. Leave the hotel. Get back to writing plays, they're harmless.

AUGUST. You're not Siri, you're one of them.

SIRI. Oh, August, come back to the real world, or you'll never see your children again.

A blackout.

Scene Four

Whispers in the dark.

Lights up.

AUGUST, *crouched by the wall, as if in conversation with his other self beyond it.*

AUGUST. 'You're a phoney.'

He hits the wall with his fist.

'You never proved anything with morphine and plants. Admit it.'

Plants have nervous systems.

'Daffodils keeled over.'

It's true!

'You're a phoney, a fraudster, you didn't prove it.'

But I know it to be true.

'Is that a scientific approach?'

Scientific discoveries depend on a balance of data and instinct.

'You mean what you want to see, you see.'

When Galileo did the mathematics for his proof that the earth and the planets go round the sun, he couldn't make them work. Time after time he redid them, but always the calculations were slightly wrong. The reason was that, though he had grasped that the planets do indeed go round the sun, he thought they did so in perfect circles. They don't – they go round the sun in ellipses. So he faked the mathematics. Because he knew he was right.

'Galileo had masses of data. What do you have?'

There is no coming to the one –

'Mumbo jumbo – '

Coming to the one –

'Mumbo jumbo – '

There is no coming to the one, with one jump –

'Alchemy mumbo jumbo – '

He shouts.

There is no coming to the one with one jump, and none, without going round about!

He is breathless, seized by a panic attack. He slumps. He holds his chest.

A pause as he calms himself.

Then the voice begins again.

'You can't – '

I can –

'You can't justify yourself – '

I am like Paracelsus! He healed people but didn't know why, there was no germ theory in the sixteenth century, he was in the dark – but his science worked –

'Paracelsus! How did he end up? A tramp, a quack, dragging himself along the road between village fairs, his books banned. That'll be your fate. It is half now, you are in exile, in Sweden they curse you, you are a pariah, *The Father* banned, *Creditors* banned, *Miss Julie* banned. The modern Paracelsus, look at you!'

He sought the Philosopher's Stone, he paid the price.

'Oh no, not the Stone thing – '

The Philosopher's Stone is made in the image of the creation of the world –

'No it's not, it's a pebble in your shoe – '

One must have the Stone's chaos and its prime matter –

'It'll cut your foot, infect your blood, reach your brain – '

The Stone is prime matter, in which the elements float hither and thither, all mixed together, until they are separated by the fiery spirit. And then –

'Then gobble-gobble-gook – '

Then there will be a blinding light.

'The ground is opening beneath you, you know it, you are sliding down into the pit. No light.'

Scene Five

FRIDA *and* AUGUST.

FRIDA. Cosy in here, poppet.

AUGUST. I like it.

FRIDA. Very August. Even the smell.

AUGUST. You came back. I thought you never would.

FRIDA. Rather obvious line for you, darling. We waved to each other very happily at the Gare de l'Est, didn't we?

AUGUST. Yes but –

FRIDA. You're experimenting again. I know I was so beastly about it, specially when we were in England. You were just getting in to it then, weren't you? The search for the Stone. It wasn't the smell, though I see – well, sniff! – that is still with you. But it was the bubbling of the glass jars –

AUGUST. Vessels, they're vessels –

FRIDA. Gurgling thingies, wobbling on top of the gas thingies –

AUGUST. Burners, Bunsen burners –

FRIDA. I was terrified they were going to explode, burn that house down. Maybe they should have, what a dreadful place that was, in that dreadful town. Gravesend.

She pulls a face.

AUGUST. Frida – why are you like this?

FRIDA. Like what, honey pie?

AUGUST. You know about alchemy, you read up on it, we talked about it for hours. You know the 'jars' are called vessels. You told me why they're that shape – bulbous, to symbolise creation. You found a painting in a book about Hieronymus Bosch, the universe as a great orb. You said he must have known about the craft. So why – childish words?

FRIDA. I'm nervous, silly. I'll do my obvious line now – 'Kiss me, you fool.'

AUGUST. I –

She embraces him but he draws back.

We can't, they're watching.

FRIDA. Who are?

AUGUST. Forces.

FRIDA. Forces.

AUGUST. I can't talk about them.

FRIDA. Creditors?

AUGUST. Worse.

FRIDA. Theatre critics?

AUGUST. I can't talk about them, I daren't!

FRIDA. Oh, August, are you imagining enemies everywhere – again?

AUGUST. There is no such thing as the imagination, things are real or they are not.

FRIDA. Well, even if they are real, they can't see in, this window's at the top of the house.

AUGUST. They're watching through the wall.

FRIDA. Then – let's give them a good show.

They look at each other.

AUGUST. That moment in Berlin. All those people, in that bar, getting louder and louder –

FRIDA. Hurly-burly –

AUGUST. Berlin arts scene! The pissed and the apocalyptic –

FRIDA. All talking at once, all about themselves – 'me me me', 'darling darling darling' –

AUGUST. Who's having whom and who's reading Nietzsche –

FRIDA. 'My gallery my book my play my hangover my last fuck' –

AUGUST. God we loved it so.

FRIDA. Didn't we.

AUGUST. Then, that's the moment.

A pause.

FRIDA. Yes.

AUGUST. You look at me.

FRIDA. You look back.

AUGUST. Silence in the bar. Everything is frozen, even the cigarette smoke in the air.

FRIDA. You're an incurable romantic, aren't you, darling.

AUGUST. I was once, but by the time of Berlin I knew I was just another dog on the street, with a cock out of control.

FRIDA. That you always were, but much more.

AUGUST. We all thought you were making a set at Munch. Edvard boasted about it. Did you ever sleep with him?

FRIDA. Now now.

AUGUST. I was tongue-tied, you so much younger, I – What did you see in me?

FRIDA. Your blue eyes.

AUGUST. Why do women say that about my eyes?

FRIDA. Don't be hypocritical, darling, you know you use them on us. And we fall for it. They are your 'come hither'.

AUGUST. Ha! I know yours.

FRIDA. Really?

AUGUST. You invite me to dinner. You assure me a fellow student would be there. He isn't. You answer the door wearing a housecoat. You open the door to me, walk across the room, slipping off the housecoat. You turn. You're wearing a slinky, moss-green dress. No corset. I see the silky green stretch over your stomach.

FRIDA. I know, it was all so bloody easy.

AUGUST. Yes. And agony.

FRIDA. Actually I wore that dress in the bar.

AUGUST. No, you wore it when I came to your apartment.

FRIDA. Oh! Deliberately for you?

AUGUST. You know you did.

FRIDA. I wore it in the bar. I'd just thrown it on that evening, and not for anyone.

AUGUST. The dress was for me, in the apartment.

FRIDA. Does it matter?

AUGUST. Of course it matters!

FRIDA. You did agonise, that first time alone. You made your excuses and left! Sometimes you are so proper, so shockable. Other times – the street dog.

A pause.

AUGUST. All right, you wore the dress in the bar. It's better in the bar. You turn, the silk tenses against you. For a moment you seem naked in public. That's more real.

FRIDA. You're not the great seducer, at all, really, are you, darling. You don't do, you like it done to you.

She takes off her coat. She is wearing the silky green dress.

A pause.

Then he embraces her.

I really didn't think this was going to happen.

They laugh.

AUGUST. Really?

FRIDA. Really, yes! I haven't shaved my legs today, do you mind?

AUGUST. No, not –

FRIDA. Bedroom?

AUGUST. In there.

FRIDA. Lovely.

She pulls him toward the door.

AUGUST. The bed's a bit –

FRIDA. If it's yours, of course it is, darling.

They kiss and begin to pull at each other's clothes.

A blackout.

Whispers.

Lights up.

AUGUST, *coming out of bedroom. He is pulling clothes back on. He speaks to the wall.*

AUGUST. Didn't see that did you? Wrong wall!

'We moved next door. She hadn't shaved her legs.'

So – what of it?

'She's sleeping with someone who likes women *au naturelle*. And we know who that is, don't we.'

She's a sensualist and a free spirit!

'But how clean is she?'

Clean?

'Clean!'

Of course she's clean.

'She's sleeping with Frank Wedekind.'

She's left me, I cannot expect –

'Wedekind is writing a play with syphilis as its hero – '

It'll never catch on –

'Something may!'

Enter FRIDA, *who listens,* AUGUST *with his back to her talking to the wall.*

'Berlin, Berlin, you are reliving Berlin – '

Why do you want to turn me against her?

'She's brash, you hate brash – '

Love and hate are interchangeable.

'Can you hate and love someone?'

Always! Love and hate!

'She's a fleeting pleasure, instant sex, illogical – '

Better illogical, sensual love than some abstract notion of domestic peace –

'Ah, the blissful moment! You pay for it, for years – '

I do pay for it! Every day!

'The memory of a fuck in a dirty Berlin room.'

Pay willingly! Because for a moment I knew I was alive!

FRIDA. You're scaring the living daylights out of me.

He turns.

She wants this, you know.

AUGUST. She –

FRIDA. Your aristo, so put upon, 'I have given him three children, he has dragged me all over Europe, I have ruined my career on the stage for him', first wife. She wants you to lose your mind.

AUGUST. I am not losing my mind.

FRIDA. No? So why are you talking to the wall?

AUGUST. Because there's someone in it.

FRIDA. Who?

AUGUST. I can't say.

FRIDA. Why not?

AUGUST. It's too dangerous.

FRIDA. Tell me who is in the fucking wall!

AUGUST. I am.

A pause.

FRIDA. August – just – try to – you know, make sense?

AUGUST. I am in the wall. Or my anti-self is. That is why he's so disgusted at what we just did.

FRIDA. Oh! This 'other you' watched us screwing? And did you turn me toward the wall, so he could get a good look at my fanny? Did he jerk off?

AUGUST. Please don't be crude.

FRIDA. It's *me* being crude here?

AUGUST. What worries me is the succubus.

FRIDA. The what?

AUGUST. The thing I'm afraid he'll send to me. It'll suck the blood out of me. And be in the form of a woman.

FRIDA. You think I'm this succubus, vampire thing?

He looks at her.

You really are scaring me now.

AUGUST. No no, you're too real, too – human.

FRIDA. Well, thank you very much, kind sir.

AUGUST. The wall told me about you and Frank Wedekind.

A pause.

FRIDA. Darling, I told you about my little thing with Frank.

AUGUST. No. The wall revealed it to me. To distress my mind.

FRIDA. No, I told you. Because we're free spirits, who love each other.

AUGUST. Free. Yes. I want that.

FRIDA. It was nothing with Frank. Oh, this is so bourgeois, the lover forced to apologise for a slight – inattention. If I have a small beer in a bar, that doesn't mean I don't want champagne with you later.

AUGUST. But it's dark, light, opposite attractions, pulling me that way, that way –

FRIDA. Oh I understand. You've always had this love/disgust thing about sex. I suppose it's being lapsed Protestant. I'm glad I'm lapsed Catholic. I know I'm going to hell and happy about it.

AUGUST. No no, you see I'm beginning to think it's not my anti-self at all.

A pause.

FRIDA. Just take stock, darling, just – (*A beat.*) This thing you're afraid will push fantasy women through the wall – is it a demon?

AUGUST. Why, yes –

FRIDA. Sent by these forces trying to stop you doing the Great Work?

AUGUST. Yes! I think I know his name – (*Whispers.*) Calipas. The enemy of alchemy, sent by Satan, to stop humanity discovering the truth of creation. (*Lower whisper.*) Though some say he's actually sent by God, to stop us meddling. (*Stops the whisper.*) The relief, Frida, that you see the great struggle I am engaged in.

FRIDA. Oh, I see the struggle... August, you must stop the alchemy.

A pause.

AUGUST. But you said you understand –

FRIDA. It's destroying you. You must abandon the experiments.

AUGUST. I am not at liberty to do that.

FRIDA. This obsession with the occult, demons in the plumbing, sending women through the wall – can't you see what's happening? The delusions are destroying your mind. Leave this hotel and come away with me. Right now.

AUGUST. Not at liberty –

FRIDA. Siri has a certificate.

A pause.

A certificate to have you put away.

AUGUST. How do you know that?

FRIDA. She told me –

AUGUST. When? Not in – the –

FRIDA. In the café.

AUGUST. You did meet!

FRIDA. Why, yes –

AUGUST. How? Did you telegram each other? Decide to gang up on me?

FRIDA. Darling, be calm –

AUGUST. Just tell me!

A pause, FRIDA *trying to judge the moment.*

FRIDA. When I left you at the Gare de l'Est I was never going to see you again. But when I got to Berlin I – you know sometimes I have this clairvoyant thing –

AUGUST. Yes, we should have done experiments –

FRIDA. No way, darling. I hate it when it happens, I'm a straightforward live-in-the-world girl, I – but on Berlin Hauptbahnhof I suddenly saw you, in this room, humiliated like the Captain at the end of your play. And I knew it was Siri. I could feel that bitch's evil, hundreds of miles away. So I never left the station, I got on a train straight back to Paris. And there she was, in the café across from the hotel entrance.

AUGUST. And you went in.

FRIDA. Yes.

AUGUST. Sat with her.

FRIDA. Yes.

AUGUST. You were laughing with her.

FRIDA. Oh, in public, women who hate each other always pretend to get on famously.

AUGUST. Laughing about me?

FRIDA. Well, you are the one thing we have in common. I had to find out what she was up to.

AUGUST. Someone said it looked like you were conspirators.

FRIDA. You mean that slut from the hotel?

AUGUST. She spoke to you, then –

FRIDA. She overheard us. She came over and said if we were talking about the gentleman in the hotel with the bad bathroom, she'd like to ask a question.

AUGUST. Which was –

FRIDA. Did we think you could make gold?

A pause.

AUGUST. And what did you say?

FRIDA. Oh yes, we said, absolutely. He can make gold.

AUGUST. Both of you said that?

FRIDA. Yes –

AUGUST. You both believe in the Great Work? That I'm not wasting my time, that I will find the Stone?

FRIDA. Course not. We played the silly girl along.

AUGUST. And you agreed, what, that you'd come up here in turns?

FRIDA. I wanted her to go first, so you could see how dangerous she is to you.

AUGUST. She's the mother of my children –

FRIDA. She wants you certified incapable.

AUGUST. Incapable –

FRIDA. Feeble of mind.

AUGUST. Yes, to destroy my will. Will is the mind's backbone, if the will is weakened, the mind crumbles.

FRIDA. Then she can have all your earnings.

He laughs.

AUGUST. What earnings?

FRIDA. Oh, you'll be really famous, darling, in the future. You know you will.

AUGUST. It's not money, it's power. I once believed in the dance of men and women, garlanded in an endless midsummer, that love was true equality. But now I know the dance is just a brawl and woman is the stronger.

FRIDA. Oh – pisscake, what nonsense, these stupid generalisations! You say things like that because the sentence scans, not because of what it means! But then you are forever the writer. And maybe you want to be tied up, tight, thrown in the back of an ambulance, committed to an asylum?

AUGUST. It would be a kind of peace. No. No, she can't win –
I must find the Stone – I have detected carbon in sulphur, the
elements are not stable –

FRIDA. None of us are 'stable' – that I learnt from you in
Berlin! Right, we leave –

AUGUST. Where to?

FRIDA. Back to Berlin, darling, where things were fun. The
Café Ferkel, remember? Where we cut free.

AUGUST. Free of our creditors –

FRIDA. Free, yes, it was wonderful! Critics in Sweden and
Norway screaming about you, Siri stirring up everyone
we knew in rages of condemnation, in Berlin we wiped the
slate clean.

AUGUST. Yes. Those weeks –

FRIDA. We had the courage to live what we preached. Free
love. Free will. (*A beat.*) So – settle your hotel bill, let Siri go
mad thumping on the café windows as we step into a taxi.

AUGUST. Actually – I can't pay the bill.

FRIDA. Oh, I'll give you money. Little else in my family,
but – there's always money. That's why they hate me being
with you!

She laughs.

AUGUST. Then we'll go.

FRIDA. Yes.

AUGUST. I must pack the vessels, the equipment, I'll need to
purchase specialist cases –

FRIDA. Junk all that stuff.

AUGUST. But –

FRIDA. There's no time.

AUGUST. But carbon *is* an attribute of sulphur! I submitted the
substance I made to the laboratory at the Sorbonne, they sent

back the analysis – 'traces of carbon'! I must have the equipment with me to continue the work –

FRIDA. I want to look after you, take you away, help you get better. I want you to be the man I saw for the first time, in the Café Ferkel – tall, broad-shouldered, radiating shyness and ferocity all at the same time.

AUGUST. I don't need to get better, there is nothing wrong with me –

FRIDA. You've lost your way.

AUGUST. I'm finding a new one.

FRIDA. I'll go down, tell them to stop a taxi for us.

AUGUST. This is my laboratory. There is a door in here, somewhere, to another world. I'll open it. And there will be the Stone.

A distortion begins. FRIDA *begins to acquire the demon's voice.*

FRIDA. Oh no, not the Stone thing.

AUGUST. The Philosopher's Stone is made in the image of the creation of the world.

FRIDA. No, it's not, it's a pebble in your shoe.

AUGUST. One must have the Stone's chaos and its prime matter.

FRIDA. It'll cut your foot, infect your blood, reach your brain.

AUGUST. The Stone is prime matter, in which the elements float hither and thither, all mixed together, until they are separated by the fiery spirit. And then –

FRIDA. Then gobble-gobble-gook.

AUGUST. Then there will be a blinding light.

FRIDA. The ground is opening beneath you, you know it, you are sliding down into the pit. No light.

The distortion ends.

A silence.

Taxi.

AUGUST. You're one of them.

FRIDA. There's a suitcase in the bedroom.

AUGUST. You're not Frida.

FRIDA. I'll throw some things in.

AUGUST. Are you the succubus?

FRIDA. We can buy you more clothes in Berlin –

AUGUST. Were you ever Frida Uhl?

FRIDA. Stop talking like this.

AUGUST. When you took me to England, were you her?

FRIDA. Stop!

AUGUST. You wanted to own me. So you took me to a country where I couldn't understand the language –

FRIDA. You are leaving with me, now.

AUGUST. English, could never stand it, that horrible whining sound.

FRIDA. Siri is coming –

AUGUST. That's why you took us to England. To erode my mind.

FRIDA. Siri is coming to this room with a –

AUGUST. You pretended you understood my scientific work but you were always undermining it –

FRIDA. It's your last chance, August.

AUGUST. Gravesend was about stopping me finding the Stone. All the time, you were sucking the life blood out of me. Wait!

FRIDA. What?

He sniffs.

AUGUST. Can't you smell it?

FRIDA. Smell –

AUGUST. There's got to be a hole, in the walls –

He runs about sniffing the walls.

FRIDA. For God's sake, what are you doing?

AUGUST. Gas, can't you smell it?

FRIDA. No.

AUGUST. The electricity didn't work, now they're trying to gas me. They'll have drilled a hole, poked through a tube –

FRIDA. Yes.

AUGUST. What?

FRIDA. It stinks.

AUGUST. You smell it?

She covers her mouth.

FRIDA. If it gets worse it'll kill us.

AUGUST. We must find the hole, block it –

FRIDA. It's poisoning us! We should get out of this room!

AUGUST. Yes.

FRIDA. Now.

AUGUST. But the gas. I must catch it, bottle it, it has to be analysed. What is its chemistry? It'll be ethereal, you see, from another dimension –

FRIDA. August! Listen! Listen! Leave with me. Prove you are sane.

A pause.

AUGUST. There was no gas. It was a trick, wasn't it, to make me stop the experiments, suck all the blood and ambition and visions out of me. You are the succubus.

A pause.

But I am Paracelsus. I will not abandon the craft.

FRIDA. It's no good. You'd better come in.

Enter SIRI *and* LOLA. LOLA *holds a straitjacket.*

AUGUST *backs away to the wall and slides down, looking up at them.*

AUGUST. No women allowed in the hotel!

FRIDA (*to* SIRI). You were right.

AUGUST. No women in the hotel!

SIRI (*to* FRIDA). I had hoped.

AUGUST. Only men allowed!

LOLA, *dangling the straitjacket.*

LOLA. Saw one of these things once in a knocking shop. Don't get me wrong – I was just cleaning.

SIRI *leans over him, then crouches, hands gently on his neck.*

SIRI. August, you have to be quiet.

AUGUST. Am I going to die?

SIRI. Oh, I think so, don't you? But I didn't plot any of this, it just – glided forward, as if on rails.

SIRI *nods to* LOLA.

LOLA. They're paying me to do this, nothing personal.

From here they get AUGUST *into the straitjacket. At first he is meek and passive.*

AUGUST. Oh, everything's personal, that's what's so wonderful about the world. Plants have feelings too, you know.

FRIDA. This is your own doing.

AUGUST. Of course! We are what we do, not what we think.
Though it's difficult – to know – exactly what you have done.

FRIDA. It was the fantastical talk, demons, making gold –

LOLA. Yeah, I knew that gold-ring thing wasn't worth spit,
where do these strings go?

SIRI. I think from his hands and round his back –

LOLA. Right.

FRIDA. Your delusions led to this end.

AUGUST. Delusions, that's what's so difficult. In the craft
nothing is certain. All is going round about. Now there are
only shadows, the other side of the furniture, only a whisper,
can shadows whisper? Yes, I can hear them, they're saying –
putrefaction not complete, putrefaction not complete –

SIRI. What's he talking about?

FRIDA. It's alchemy crap – everything must putrefy before it
can re-emerge in a different form. I boned up on it when we
were in England, to chivvy him along.

SIRI. We both did our chivvying.

FRIDA. Yes, that's all over now.

AUGUST. Can I have something to rest my head?

SIRI (*to* LOLA). Get him a pillow.

LOLA. If there's going to be sex when he's tied up, I'm asking
for extra.

She exits.

AUGUST. Make it tight, I deserve it.

FRIDA. Don't worry, darling. And when the ambulance comes,
you'll be at peace.

*LOLA enters with a striped – and rather stained – pillow.
She puts it behind his head.*

AUGUST. Thank you. I'm cold.

SIRI. Here.

She puts her shawl over him.

AUGUST. Siri, your shawl, it's – soft on my mouth. Smooth, warm, like your arm it – smells of vanilla. Like you did when you were young – and we walked in the birch woods – how beautiful life was! And now it's like this. Do you want it like this? I truly don't. Yet here we are. Who rules our lives?

LOLA. God rules our lives.

And he's on the attack.

AUGUST. Ah! A whore with religion!

LOLA. Talk to me like that, I'll give you a good kicking!

AUGUST. Oh yes, kick me, now I'm helpless! Come on, all of you, why not? And get this thing off me! It stinks, it's poisoned, like Medea's cloak!

SIRI *whisks the shawl away.*

From here LOLA *loses interest and sits in a corner on the floor. She eats apples.*

And cut these strings.

SIRI. Don't be silly, you know you want this.

AUGUST. How can I possibly want it?

SIRI. Because it's good for you.

AUGUST. No good here –

FRIDA. My lover, my flame from Berlin, it's good for you because it's an experience.

AUGUST. No no no, get it off!

SIRI. Sad how they *say* they want experience then chicken out.

FRIDA. Run a mile at the real thing.

SIRI. Like he ran from us.

AUGUST. I didn't run from you, you ran from me. (*To* SIRI.) You to the arms of that woman! (*To* FRIDA.) You back to your rich family.

SIRI. You ran from me because I slept with a woman.

FRIDA. You ran from me because I slept with another writer.

AUGUST. Frank Wedekind. How could you? He's a Communist and – German!

FRIDA. You're jealous because he plays the guitar better than you.

AUGUST. 'Epic theatre', so superficial. Wedekind? Keep journalists out of theatre. True drama has no message.

FRIDA. Shall I tell you a secret? Though it won't be one for much longer. It will begin to show.

AUGUST. No –

FRIDA. Yes, darling, I'm carrying Wedekind's child.

AUGUST. No –

FRIDA. You sprayed the head of Frank's baby.

AUGUST. No, not that.

FRIDA (*to* SIRI). It's always disgusted him, that idea.

SIRI. Makes him squeamish.

FRIDA. Throw up at the thought.

SIRI. Other men's babies inside us.

FRIDA. Are all your children his?

SIRI. He wonders. Don't you, dear.

He looks from one to another.

A pause.

AUGUST (*low*). Can't bear –

FRIDA. What?

SIRI. What?

AUGUST. I cannot bear infidelity!

SIRI. Oh!

FRIDA. Oh!

SIRI. Who was that fifteen-year-old at Skovlyst?

AUGUST. She was sixteen, she lied about her age to get money out of me – and it was – Midsummer's Night.

SIRI. Oh, another Midsummer's Night, why are they meant to make everything forgiven?

FRIDA. And there was that dazzler at Café Ferkel. I know you had her.

AUGUST (*to* SIRI). And your lesbian – person. I cannot bear the thought, I'm a family man.

FRIDA. She may be a family girl.

AUGUST. But she's – she's –

FRIDA (*to* SIRI). Here it comes, he's going to say it –

AUGUST. She's –

SIRI. Yes, what is she?

FRIDA. Squeeze a liberal hard enough and, like puss out of a boil, out pops the antisemitism.

AUGUST. I am no antisemite and I am certainly no liberal!

SIRI. Oh, August, if only you realised how ordinary you really are.

A pause.

LOLA. Is the sex going to get going yet?

AUGUST (*to* SIRI). It wasn't the love affairs. The court case destroyed our marriage.

She stares at him.

SIRI. Here we go, his famous court case.

FRIDA. Brings it up sooner or later.

SIRI. I was ill, little Hans was ill, but oh no, the man's reputation comes before all! So you left us, didn't you, darling, stranded in Switzerland.

AUGUST. I had to go back! I was a hero for the cause.

FRIDA. 'A hero for the cause'! Listen to him, the phoney trumpeting of the self-aggrandising male –

AUGUST. It wasn't phoney, it was horribly real, I was accused of blasphemy!

SIRI. It was just theatre to you. A great opportunity for bad acting on the steps of the High Court.

AUGUST. 'Blasphemy against God or mockery against God's holy words and sacraments.' That was the charge. I faced two years in prison. All because I wrote a little story!

SIRI. Dirty little story.

FRIDA. *Getting Married* – actually, I loved that book.

SIRI (*to* FRIDA). You weren't in it, I was.

AUGUST (*to* FRIDA). When you first read it you said it was wonderful.

FRIDA. Chivvying?

SIRI. Chivvying.

AUGUST. My sin was the book was popular! The Crown Bitch read it and decided to destroy me. Alerted the public prosecutor.

FRIDA. 'Crown Bitch', can he possibly mean the Queen of Sweden?

AUGUST. She set the public prosecutor on me. Women are the worst reactionaries.

SIRI. Says the champion of women's rights.

AUGUST. I was your champion! My manifesto for the equality of the sexes –

SIRI. Which the Stockholm feminists hated.

AUGUST. I was too radical for them!

FRIDA. Ha! (*Gestures toward him in his straitjacket.*) I give
you a man more feminist than the feminists.

AUGUST. It was a cabal of upper-class women, resentful of
a man from the lower classes with the cheek to lead their
cause. Just a bunch of jealous bitches.

LOLA. Ah, right, right, I get it! You're bloody intellectuals, all
talk, no sex.

FRIDA. For him, this is sex.

LOLA. Dearie me.

SIRI *kneels beside him. Now they talk intimately.*

SIRI. You came back after the trial, wrecked.

AUGUST. I won.

SIRI. You lost.

AUGUST. I was acquitted.

SIRI. Your mind was soured.

AUGUST. Soured?

SIRI. You felt humiliated.

AUGUST. My country tried to silence me!

SIRI. You sharpened your claws, you began to attack the
women's movement.

AUGUST. They didn't support me during the trial!

SIRI. You wanted revenge – on Sweden, on your old radical
friends, on women. You became savage and cruel in everything
you wrote. You drank, took drugs, turned to all kinds of
extreme thoughts. God, Schopenhauer? Please. Then –

A pause.

Then you turned on me. Suspicions, ravings, writing to acquaintances asking them to spy on me. And it broke us. And now – you've turned on your own talent, ruined your mind with this – false science. And here you are. At the bottom of an inferno of your own making.

A pause.

AUGUST. You were my true love.

SIRI. You were mine.

AUGUST. One and true love.

SIRI. Yes.

FRIDA. What about me in all this?

SIRI. You were just a fuck on the side.

FRIDA. How dare you!

AUGUST. She's right, you were a fuck on the side.

FRIDA *turns away, turns back.*

FRIDA. I wanted to rescue you.

SIRI. Beyond rescue.

AUGUST. Go back to Berlin. Where you belong.

SIRI. In the cigarette smoke.

FRIDA. Everything Daddy said about you is true. Do you know what he calls you?

AUGUST. 'Degenerate'?

FRIDA. Worse.

AUGUST. 'Enemy of Society'?

FRIDA. Far worse. He calls you 'arty farty'. Perhaps that's what you are. (*A beat.*) I'll never forget you.

SIRI. No. You'll go on lecture tours, telling lies about your days with the great writer.

FRIDA. Stories. Goodbye, August.

She exits.

AUGUST. You've taken my strength.

SIRI. Yes.

AUGUST. You'll leave me like this?

SIRI. Yes.

AUGUST. The certificate –

SIRI. Oh, it's branded on your forehead now, for ever. Madman. Woman hater.

She kisses his forehead and exits.

LOLA *takes out another apple and begins to eat it.*

AUGUST. When putrefaction is ended and all is black, and molten and formless, then the master of the craft begins the seven operations of the Great Work.

A beat.

First: calcination. To burn away dross, reveal hidden essences.

A beat.

Then dissolution. Breaking down of the artificial structures of the psyche.

A beat.

Third stage: separation. By filtration, separate out the shadowy materials of things of which we are ashamed.

A beat.

Fourth: conjunction. A coming-together, beyond thought or feeling, the glimpse of a new reality.

A beat.

Fifth of the seven operations: fermentation. And putrefaction has gone, a white layer appears, new life.

A beat.

Sixth: distillation. The purification of the unborn self.

A beat.

Then at last: the seventh operation.

A beat.

Coagulation. The transformation of what was base, and dull, and compromised, ambiguous, into incorruptible gold. And the soul returns to the Garden of Eden, in a blinding light.

A beat.

And you are free.

He pulls the straitjacket off him and throws it across the room.

LOLA. Liked that, did you?

He is dead still.

I weren't actually gonna do knots on that thing. I've seen kinky games go wrong. Very wrong. Not that I've – y'know, this kind of thing – often.

He is still dead still.

Right, mister, where's my gold?

She throws the apple at him. He flinches.

It's Tuesday, where's my gold?

AUGUST. Yes. Yes.

He holds out both hands then, with a palming movement, he produces a gold ring.

LOLA. Aunt Ada –

She slips it on her finger. She holds it up.

They'll make you pay for this.

AUGUST. Who, the forces?

LOLA. Police, all of 'em. Making gold out of nothing? What'll banks think of that, the government? You could wreck the world.

AUGUST. That's – most perceptive of you.

LOLA. Ooh my –

AUGUST. Bright.

LOLA. Bright yes, ooh! But then I'm a bright girl, you lot just don't see it.

AUGUST. My lot?

LOLA. Educated la-de-dahs.

AUGUST. Ah. (*A beat.*) We educated la-di-das, we have the notion that the world must be – one.

She looks at him for a moment.

LOLA. You mean everything must be like everything else?

AUGUST. Yes! Plants, animals evolve and so must metals, chemicals, which means that the elements are not stable. They can be transmuted. Changed. And that has a vast moral implication, it means we can change our natures, a kind of – alchemy of the spirit – break ourselves down, rebuild, be new. In the light.

LOLA. Sorry?

AUGUST. I babble.

LOLA. God, don't you! Still, the babble works. It made this.

She holds up the ring.

AUGUST. Look closer.

She does.

LOLA. Oh. There're little black spots –

AUGUST. In a few days it'll all be black. You can freshen it up, get some tweezers and hold it in a gas flame.

LOLA. Tweezers? Well, ta for nothing.

AUGUST. So you can go back in the wall now.

LOLA. What you mean, wall? Back downstairs, that's where I'm going, turn you in to the management.

AUGUST. I'm getting rid of it all. The laboratory equipment. I'll dump it in the bins in the courtyard. And I'll clean the bath.

A pause.

LOLA. Give me ten francs and I'll do it for you.

AUGUST. Done. *Miss Julie*'s opened in Bern, there'll be royalties at the bank.

LOLA. Miss Who?

AUGUST. A play.

LOLA. Play? You in the theatre?

AUGUST. Yeah. (*A beat.*) Sometimes I try not to be, but I am.

LOLA. Well, that explains a lot – getting yourself tied up, shouting at people who aren't there.

AUGUST. That what I've –

LOLA. Oh yeah! Some guests have complained, some have had a good laugh about you.

AUGUST. I must apologise –

LOLA. Don't bother, most of 'em are out of their heads too.

She eyes him. A hiatus.

AUGUST. Well –

LOLA. I've got a bit of a voice, y'know.

AUGUST. Have you now.

LOLA. I do a comic song now and then at The Olympia, on the early-evening programme. I'm not much of a singer but I can, y'know –

She moves her hips, laughs.

AUGUST. The Olympia's not quite my kind of theatre –

LOLA. No, I was thinking about acting, do you give lessons? I can't pay much, but y'know, I'm very keen.

AUGUST. Oh God, help me. I do believe I'm sane again. Well, my dear, I could. What's your name?

A distortion. Her voice suddenly of the demon.

LOLA. You know my name.

AUGUST. I thought I was free of you.

LOLA. Never.

AUGUST. You won't win.

LOLA. We always win.

AUGUST. Every town I go to, from now on, I'll go to its asylum, stand outside its wall and swear I will never end up on the other side.

LOLA. It'll do no good.

AUGUST. I'll write a play, to drive you down into the earth, forever.

LOLA (*demonic sneer*). Yes. You'll call it *To Damascus* and it won't work.

AUGUST. It will.

LOLA. It'll be a disaster, totally bloody unperformable, darling. Just like the alchemy.

Distortion ends.

Harriet.

He stares at her.

That's my name. When you meet me, seven years from now, I'll be younger. Twenty-three years old. I'll become your third wife. And I will give you absolute hell.

End of play.

A Nick Hern Book

The Blinding Light first published in Great Britain as a paperback original in 2017 by Nick Hern Books Limited, The Glasshouse, 49a Goldhawk Road, London W12 8QP, in association with Jermyn Street Theatre, London

The Blinding Light copyright © 2017 Howard Brenton

Howard Brenton has asserted his right to be identified as the author of this work

Cover image: Visual Things

Designed and typeset by Nick Hern Books, London
Printed in the UK by Mimeo Ltd, Huntingdon, Cambridgeshire PE29 6XX

A CIP catalogue record for this book is available from the British Library

ISBN 9781 84842 706 8

www.nickhernbooks.co.uk

facebook.com/nickhernbooks

twitter.com/nickhernbooks